Spell of Steam

By the same author
Steam Up
Lure of Steam
Portrait of Steam
Glory of Steam
Main Lines Across the Border
(in conjunction with O.S. Nock)

Eric Treacy

Spell of Steam

LONDON
IAN ALLAN LTD

First published 1973

Second impression 1974

ISBN O 7110 0457 9

© Eric Treacy, 1973

Published by Ian Allan Ltd, Shepperton, Surrey
and printed in the United Kingdom
by Ian Allan (Printing) Ltd.

Contents

Introduction

I suppose that I could start this Introduction by quoting Tommy Handley's wartime radio programme: "It's that man again". For I recall that I have said about previous books which have been published, "this is my last".

You could also say about many of the photographs in this book: "It's that picture again". And you would be right! That is, in part, the justification of this book.

Some time ago, Geoffrey Freeman Allen suggested to me that there might be a market for another book from me containing the best of my work over the last forty years, together with a certain amount of new material, much of it from the preserved lines.

I realise that the word 'best', in this context, is a matter of opinion. Obviously, it means what is 'best' to me, which is a subjective judgement. I can only hope that there will be some who will share my judgement as to what constitutes my best work.

I have included pictures from *Steam Up* published in 1948, and long out of print; from *Main Lines Across the Border* (Nelson), in which I collaborated with O. S. Nock; and a number from my recent books, *Lure, Portrait* and *Glory of Steam* (all Ian Allan). I have done my best to set out the pictures so that they are not crowded. If I may say so, there are a few 'repeats' here to which justice has never been done in previous books. The photograph of the wartime 'Royal Scot' on page 11 is an example of this.

Well, there it is. An offering from a steam lover to others who hold precious the memories of the days when those grunting, noisy, dirty, temperamental, but splendid monsters held sway on the British railway system.

Perhaps the day will come, as Sir Gerald Nabarro has forecast, that some genius, when the oil supplies of the world have run out, will invent a steam engine. When, and if, that happens, I hope these pictures may give our hypothetical inventor some ideas to work on.

Left: A1 Pacific No 60152 *Holyrood* leaves Edinburgh Waverley with a train for Carlisle.

Below: Two Bishops on the footplate. Leonard Wilson (Bishop of Birmingham) right, and Eric Treacy (Bishop of Wakefield) left, on the occasion of the naming at Tyseley of Black 5 No 5428 *Eric Treacy*. The ceremony was performed by the Bishop of Birmingham. /*Birmingham Post*

Railway Atmosphere

Above: Rousing start at Lochty. Preserved A4 Pacific No 60009 *Union of South Africa* sets out for Knightsward.

Right: Pounding up the hill from Lime Street, un-rebuilt Scot No 6130 *West Yorkshire Regiment* heads an express for Euston.

Below: Wartime on Shap. The down 'Royal Scot' picks up after being stopped at the home signal at Shap Wells. Stanier Pacific No 6234 *Duchess of Abercorn* is in charge.

Above: Almost at the top, Jubilee 4-6-0 No 45573 *Newfoundland* approaches Ais Gill Summit on the Settle-Carlisle line with the up 'Waverley' express.

Above: Lime Street cutting. Princess Royal Pacific No 46208 *Princess Helena Victoria* blasts up the hill from Lime Street Station with the up 'Shamrock'.

Right: Stormy morning at Fort William. K2 2-6-0 No 61787 *Loch Quoich* leaves for Mallaig.

Top left: A Patriot 4-6-0 climbs Shap at Greenholme with a northbound freight.

Left: A Stanier Black 5 pilots a Stanier Jubilee 4-6-0 near Ais Gill with a Leeds to Glasgow Express.

Above: 15 mph at Harthope. Princess Royal Pacific No 46210 *Lady Patricia* struggles unassisted to Beattock Summit with the Birmingham 'Scotsman'.

Right: The perfect location—one more in the cutting of Edge Hill. Rebuilt Scot No 46124 *London Scottish* is Euston-bound with the up 'Merseyside Express'.

Bottom right: Surely Britain's most handsome steam locomotive. Stanier Pacific No 46255 *City of Hereford,* photographed on a summer's evening at Crewe North shed.

Below: Sunshine and shadow in Newcastle Central. A3 Pacific No 60037 *Hyperion* about to leave for Edinburgh with the down 'Flying Scotsman'.

The Great 20th Century CMEs

Above: A Royal Scot before rebuilding. No 46110 *Grenadier Guardsman* at Wreay with the Birmingham 'Scotsman'.

Top right: Stanier Jubilee 4-6-0 No 45593 *Kolhapur* in Holbeck shed.

Right: Two Stanier Black 5s at Ais Gill with the up 'Waverley' express.

Above: One of Stanier's streamlined Pacifics, No 6223 *Princess Alice*, climbs to Shap Summit at Thrimby with the up 'Coronation Scot'.

Below: Rebuilt Patriot No 45527 *Southport* passes Edge Hill No 2 box with the up 'Merseyside Express'.

A1 Pacific No 60162 *St Johnstoun* leaves Carlisle with a train for Edinburgh
via the Waverley route.

No 45500 *Patriot,* in the original Fowler version of the class, leaves
Carnforth with the up 'Lakes Express'.

Leaving Shrewsbury for Crewe is Stanier Pacific No 46255 *City of Hereford* with a West of England train for Manchester and Liverpool.

Below: The first rebuilt Royal Scot engine to be fitted with smoke deflectors. No 6115 *Scots Guardsman* at Chester with 'horse and carriage' train.

Right: Another Stanier Princess Royal Pacific No 46201 *Princess Elizabeth* at Clifton, near Penrith, with the southbound Birmingham 'Scotsman'.

Bottom right: One of Stanier's streamlined Pacifics with casing removed. No 46229 *Duchess of Hamilton* showing cut-away smokebox door, at Carlisle.

Above: Gresley A3 Pacific No 61 *Pretty Polly* at Peascliffe, near Grantham, with a train from Leeds to Kings Cross.

Below: Gresley A4 Pacific No 60031 *Golden Plover* in the woods at Penmanshiel with an express from Glasgow to Kings Cross.

Left: Peppercorn A1 Pacific No 60141 *Abbotsford* passes Wortley South with the up 'Queen of Scots' Pullman.

Above: One of Gresley's V2 general purpose 2-6-2s, No 60978, approaches Newcastle Central with freight.

Right: Peppercorn A1 Pacific No 60117 *Bois Roussel* leaves Copley Hill shed for duty on the up 'Yorkshire Pullman'. Note flared chimney which greatly improved the appearance of these engines.

Left: Gresley K2 2-6-0 No 61791 *Loch Laggan* leaves Fort William with the morning train for Mallaig.

Bottom left: Thompson B1 4-6-0 No 61016 *Inyala* pilots a V2 2-6-2 out of Leeds City with a train for Newcastle.

Below: Introduced by Thompson in 1946, A2/3 Pacific No 60519 *Honeyway* at Carlisle with a train for Edinburgh Waverley.

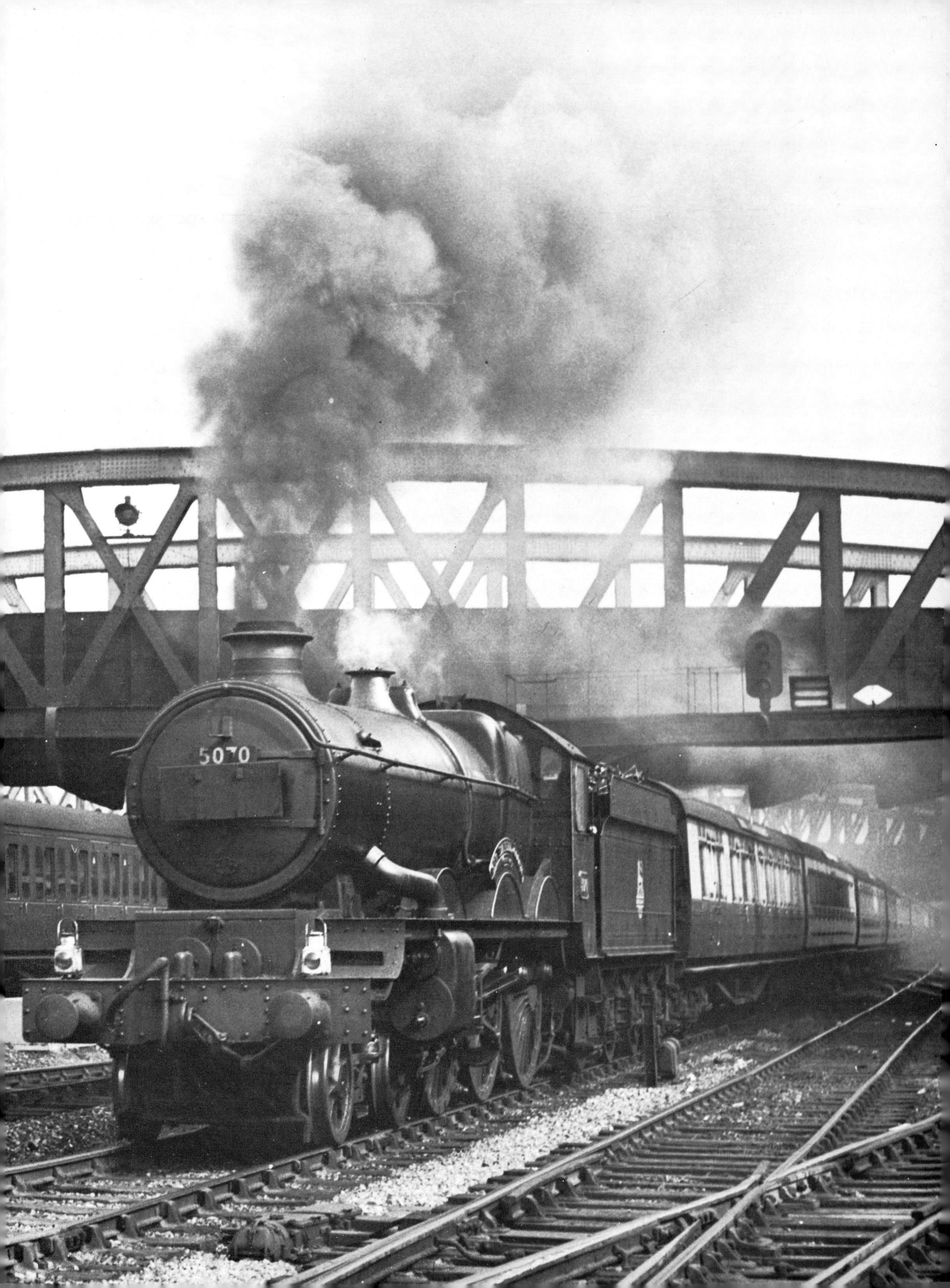
5070

Left: Collett Castle class 4-6-0 No 5070 *Sir Daniel Gooch* leaves Paddington with a train for Plymouth.

Right: Collett King class 4-6-0 No 6028 *King George VI* at Old Oak Common.

Below: Maunsell Schools class 4-4-0 No 910 *Merchant Taylors* north of Tonbridge with a train from Hastings to London.

Above: One of Bulleid's early West Country class Pacifics, No 21C 139, labours up the bank from Victoria to the Grosvenor Bridge.

Below: Maunsell Lord Nelson 4-6-0 No 854 *Howard of Effingham* leaves Victoria with morning boat train.

Above: Maunsell Class N15 (King Arthur) 4-6-0 No 784 *Sir Nerovens* leaves Salisbury with a train for Waterloo.

Left: Bulleid Battle of Britain Pacific No 34082 *615 Squadron* coaling at Nine Elms shed.

Famous Expresses

The 'Merseyside Express'. Princess Royal Pacific No 46208 *Princess Helena Victoria* slogs up Camden Bank out of Euston with the down train.

The 'Royal Scot'. The down train photographed at Harthope on Beattock bank behind Pacific No 46250 *City of Lichfield.*

Above: The 'Irish Mail'. The up 'Mail' leaves Holyhead behind rebuilt Scot No 46146 *The Rifle Brigade.*

Below: The 'Coronation Scot'. Summer's evening on Shap as streamlined Pacific No 6222 *Queen Mary* makes the climb.

Above: The 'Red Rose'. The up train at Wavertree behind Pacific No 46202 *Princess Anne,* rebuilt from the LMS Turbomotive.

Top right: The 'White Rose'. A1 Pacific No 60114 *W.P. Allen* leaves Leeds Central for Kings Cross.

Right: The 'Golden Arrow'. Britannia Pacific No 70004 *William Shakespeare* framed at Victoria.

Left: The 'Caledonian'. Pacific No 46239 *City of Chester* passes Camden sheds with the down train.

Bottom left: The 'Flying Scotsman'. A4 Pacific No 60008 *Dwight D. Eisenhower* at York on a December day in 1948.

Below: The 'Devon Belle'. A Merchant Navy Pacific rounds the bend from Waterloo with the onetime Pullman for the Devon coast.

The 'Queen of Scots' Pullman. A1 Pacific No 60126 *Sir Vincent Raven* heads for Edinburgh from Leeds Central, where the train has reversed.

Right: The 'Elizabethan'. A4 Pacific No 60022 *Mallard* at Portobello East.

Below: The 'Tees-Tyne Pullman'. A4 Pacific No 60014 *Silver Link* storms out of Kings Cross.

The 'Thames-Clyde Express'. The down train at Wortley Junction, Leeds, hauled by rebuilt Scot No 46108 *Seaforth Highlander*.

The 'Waverley' express. Two Jubilee 4-6-0s leave Hellifield at the foot of the climb to Blea Moor.

Top left: The 'Irish Mail'. The up 'Mail' at Bethesda Junction, Bangor; Class 2P 4-4-0 pilots Royal Scot No 6112 *Sherwood Forester.*

Left: The 'Midday Scot'. Under storm clouds at Great Strickland Pacific No 46247 *City of Liverpool* makes for Shap Summit.

Above: The 'Yorkshire Pullman'. A gleaming A4, No 60034 *Lord Faringdon,* emerges from Gas Works Tunnel, Kings Cross, with the down train.

The Waverley Route

Above: A3 Pacific No 60079 *Bayardo* (note right-hand drive) leaves Carlisle Citadel with the 'Waverley' express, bound for Edinburgh.

Top right: Freight train at Newcastleton, headed by K3/3 2-6-0 No 61878.

Right: Scene at Canal Junction north of Carlisle. Class A2/1 Pacific No 60507 *Highland Chieftain* backs down to Citadel station for the down 'Waverley' while WD 2-8-0 No 90505 does some shunting.

A freight train leaving Hawick for
Carlisle behind K3/2 2-6-0 No 61968

Left: The up 'Waverley' express near Shankend headed by A3 Pacific No 60093 *Coronach.*

Below: Class B1 4-6-0 No 61290 climbs through Stobs station to Riccarton with a freight train.

Right: Class K3/2 2-6-0 No 61876 approaches Falahill Summit with a freight train for Millerhill.

Below: Scene in the locomotive yards at Hawick station.

Weekend in Paris

Above: Chapelon Pacific No 231 E 31 at La Chappelle shed, Paris.

Right: No 141 TC 25, a 2-8-2T, takes water at the Gard du Nord.

Left: Two Chapelon Pacifics at La Chappelle shed.

Below: Chapelon Pacific No 231 E 31 ready for duty at La Chappelle shed.

'Golden Arrow'

Britannia Pacific No 70004 *William Shakespeare* leaves Victoria with the
down 'Golden Arrow'.

The down 'Golden Arrow' climbs out of Victoria, headed by Bulleid Battle of
Britain Pacific No 21C 157.

French edition of the 'Golden Arrow' about to leave Calais for Paris behind
Chapelon Pacific No 231 E 44.

BR Standard Locomotives

The down 'Thames-Clyde Express' leaves Leeds City station en route for
Glasgow, headed by Britannia Class Pacific No 70016 *Ariel*.

Top left: Class 4MT 4-6-0 No 75030 passes Camden sheds with a local train for Bletchley.

Left: Standard Class 5 4-6-0 No 73171 leaves York with a local train for Leeds.

Above: Britannia Pacific No 70050 *Firth of Clyde* passes Harrison's Lime Works, near Shap, with a train from Glasgow to Manchester.

Right: Clan Pacific No 72002 *Clan Campbell* at Scout Green with a train from Manchester to Glasgow.

Hills of the North

Above: Beattock. The down 'Royal Scot' at Greskine, headed by Stanier Pacific No 46240 *City of Coventry.*

Top right: Shap. Royal Scot No 6156 *South Wales Borderer* heads the down 'Royal Scot' at Shap Wells—'15 on and steam to spare'.

Right: Settle to Blea Moor. Class 5 4-6-0 No 44755, fitted with Caprotti valve gear, takes the down 'Waverley' express to the top. Pen-y-Ghent is in the background.

Top left: Shap. Two bankers from Tebay wait at the summit before returning for duty at Tebay.

Left: Beattock. The down 'Royal Scot' at Harthope headed by Princess Royal Pacific No 46201 *Princess Elizabeth.*

Above: The down 'Thames-Clyde Express' in Ribblesdale, headed by Britannia Pacific No 70053 *Moray Firth.*

Beattock. Class 6 No 72003 *Clan Fraser* at Longbedholm with a Perth train.

Top left: Shap. Jubilee 4-6-0 No 5592 *Indore* nears the summit with a freight train.

Left: Ais Gill. 'Crab' 2-6-0 No 42816 under the shadow of Wild Boar Fell with a southbound freight.

Above: Ribblehead. Class 5 4-6-0 No 45013 drifts down the hill under the flank of Whernside with a freight train.

Left: Beattock. The up 'Royal Scot' at Crawford behind Pacific No 46223 *Princess Alice.*

Bottom left: Shap. The up 'Coronation Scot' at Clifton, headed by streamlined Pacific No 6224 *Princess Alexandra.*

Right: Carlisle to Settle. Two Jubilee 4-6-0s pound through the Eden Valley at Armathwaite with the up 'Thames-Clyde Express'.

Below: Bell Busk. A Morecambe train headed by Compound 4-4-0 No 1006 and a Class 4 0-6-0.

Above: Shap. Princess Royal Pacific No 46210 *Lady Patricia* pounds to the summit with a Birmingham to Glasgow train.

Below: Shap. In the days of the LMS. Royal Scot 4-6-0 No 6109 *Royal Engineer* at Clifton with a train from Perth.

Left: Penrith. Class 5 4-6-0 No 45316 with a northbound freight train.

Bottom left: Dent. The down 'Thames-Clyde Express' passes Dent station behind rebuilt Royal Scot 4-6-0 No 46103 *Royal Scots Fusilier.*

Below: Beattock. Jubilee Class 4-6-0 No 45674 *Duncan* at Longbedholm with a Manchester to Glasgow train.

Penrith. In its original form, Stanier Pacific No 6232 *Duchess of Montrose* heads the up 'Mid-day Scot'.

Clifton. Class G2A 0-8-0 No 9120 rounds the curve with a freight train.

A Class WD 'Austerity' 2-8-0 at Ribblesdale with limestone 'tipplers'.

Above: Class 8F 2-8-0 No 8080 at Marley Junction, near Keighley, with northbound freight.

Left: At Kingmoor, Carlisle, Class 5 4-6-0 No 45169 brings in a freight train from Scotland.

Right: A northbound freight leaves Kingmoor behind Jubilee 4-6-0 No 45677 *Beatty*.

Left: Class WD 'Austerity' 2-8-0 at Wakefield, bound for Healey Mills with a coal train.

Below: At Abington. Drummond Caledonian 0-6-0 No 57451 with a 'pick-up' goods train on the Glasgow-Carlisle main line.

Glasgow and South Western

Class 2P 4-4-0 No 40593 leaves Kilmarnock with a stopping train to Dumfries.

Above: Standard Class 5 4-6-0 No 73063 at Carronbridge with a northbound freight.

Top right: In the Nith Valley. Drummond Caledonian 0-6-0 No 57571 at Thornhill with a freight train.

Right: More in the Nith Valley. A Crab 2-6-0 trots along with southbound freight.

Sheds

Above: York South. Two 4-6-0s—left, B1 No 61124; and right Jubilee
No 45594 *Bhopal.*

Top right: Copley Hill. Class J6 0-6-0 No 64277 (right) and A1 Pacific
No 60123 *H.A. Ivatt* (left).

Right: Edge Hill. Stanier Pacific No 6254 *City of Stoke-on-Trent* and Class 5
4-6-0 No 5025.

Copley Hill. Class A3 Pacific No 60056 *Centenary.*

Camden. Left to right: Rebuilt Scot No 46115 *Scots Guardsman,* Princess Pacific No 46208 *Princess Helena Victoria* and rebuilt Scot No 46138 *London Irish Rifleman.*

Holbeck. Jubilee 4-6-0 No 45593 *Kolhapur.*

Below: Nine Elms. The driver lights up whilst his Bulleid Pacific takes water.

Right: Nine Elms. During the locomotive exchanges of 1948, Class A4 Pacific No 60022 *Mallard* visits Nine Elms, and stands by a Lord Nelson 4-6-0.

Bottom right: Haymarket. At the west end of the shed, Peppercorn A2 Pacific No 60535 *Hornet's Beauty* and K3/2 2-6-0 No 61987.

Left: Holbeck. Class 9F 2-10-0 No 92026 fitted with Franco-Crosti boiler.

Below: Holbeck. Class 9F 2-10-0 No 92026 moves on to the turntable.

Top left: Doncaster. A young fireman reports for work under the watchful eye of A1 Pacific No 60149 *Amadis.*

Left: York. End of the shift—an engineman homeward bound.

Above: York. A breakdown crane re-rails an ex-NER 4-4-0 in the York south yards.

Holbeck. Group of engines in the roundhouse.

Derby. Jubilee 4-6-0 No 45618 *New Hebrides* and Standard Class 5
4-6-0 No 73069.

Stations

Kings Cross. The down 'Tees-Tyne Pullman' leaves for Newcastle behind
Class A4 Pacific No 60022 *Mallard.*

Above: Leeds City. A Liverpool to Newcastle train leaves behind Class D49/2 4-4-0 No 62749 *The Cottesmore* and A3 Pacific No 60074 *Harvester.*

Below: York. A Newcastle to Kings Cross train headed by Class A3 Pacific No 60091 *Captain Cuttle.*

Above: Leeds City. Pollution! Jubilee 4-6-0 No 45595 *Southern Rhodesia* pilots rebuilt Royal Scot No 46124 *London Scottish* on a Newcastle to Liverpool train.

Top right: Leeds Central. A3 Pacific No 56 *Centenary* leaves with a mid-day train for Kings Cross.

Right: Kings Cross. Approaching 10am, the 'Flying Scotsman' waits for the green flag. At the head is Class A1 Pacific No 60133.

Top left: Edinburgh Princes Street. Pickersgill 4-4-0 No 54503 leaves with a local train.

Left: Glasgow Central. The up 'Midday Scot' sets out for Euston behind Princess Royal Pacific No 46205 *Princess Victoria.*

Above: Paddington. Britannia Pacific No 70027 *Rising Star* leaves with a train for Cardiff. On the left is Castle 4-6-0 No 5063 *Earl Baldwin.*

Left: Hildenborough, Kent. A down boat train behind Bulleid West Country Pacific No 21C 138 passes a typical country station.

Bottom left: Sheffield Park. Another country station; ex-SECR 0-6-0 No 27 with a train on the Bluebell Railway.

Below: Liverpool Lime Street. Jubilee 4-6-0 No 45646 *Napier* sets out with a train for Hull.

Above: Victoria. Bulleid West Country Pacific No 34038 *Lynton* leaves for the Kent Coast.

Below: Newcastle. The down 'Flying Scotsman' departs for Edinburgh behind Class A4 Pacific No 60012 *Commonwealth of Australia.*

Above: Ex-L&Y 0-6-0 No 12619 heads south from Preston.

Top right: Class B1 4-6-0 No 61320 creeps into the goods yard at Ardsley, near Wakefield.

Right: Class 5 4-6-0 No 45122 coasts down the hill from Beattock Summit.

Top left: Jubilee 4-6-0 No 45593 *Kolhapur* leaves Bradford Forster Square with a fitted freight train for Heysham. This was taken on the last day of steam working from Bradford.

Left: In the valley of the Lune. Crab 2-6-0 No 42786 heads into storm clouds over the Howgill Fells, at Low Gill.

Above: Jubilee 4-6-0 No 45596 *Bahamas* (before fitting of double chimney) moves away from Penrith with southbound freight.

Changing Scene at Edinburgh Waverley

Above: Class A3 Pacific No 60090 *Grand Parade* waits to leave with the up 'Queen of Scots' Pullman.

Top right: Class A4 Pacific No 60004 *William Whitelaw* leaves Edinburgh Waverley with a Glasgow-Kings Cross train.

Right: Two station pilots at Edinburgh Waverley. Holmes NB Class J83 0-6-0Ts Nos 68474 and 68477.

Left: A Glasgow to Kings Cross train leaves Waverley behind A4 Pacific No 60010 *Dominion of Canada.*

Bottom left: A1 Pacific No 60160 *Auld Reekie* at the west end of Waverley with the Glasgow-bound 'North Briton'.

Below: Class J83 0-6-0T No 68481 shunts empty stock—in spite of express train headlamps!

Below: Framed in North British cast iron, Deltic No 9018 *Ballymoss* at the head of the up 'Flying Scotsman'.

Right: Class A2 Pacific No 60529 *Pearl Diver* sets out from Waverley with the up 'Queen of Scots' Pullman.

Some Tank Engines

Above: Class 3MT 2-6-2T No 73 at Bathesda Junction with a local train from Llandudno Junction to Bangor.

Right: Class N2 0-6-2T No 69492 with empty stock approaches Copenhagen Tunnel, Kings Cross.

Above: Derby station. Class 2MT 2-6-2T No 41247 arrives with a train from Birmingham.

Left: The morning 'pick-up' from Beattock to Moffat, headed by Class 4 2-6-4T No 42205.

Castles and Kings

Locomotive Exchanges, 1948. King 4-6-0 No 6019 *King Henry V* at Beeston
with the morning train from Leeds to Kings Cross.

Left: Castle class No 4079 *Pendennis Castle* at Chester.

Below: Castle class 4-6-0 No 4079 *Pendennis Castle* is serviced at Chester mpd on the occasion of an Ian Allan excursion to Birkenhead.

Above: Another shot of No 4079 *Pendennis Castle* at Chester on an
Ian Allan excursion.

Top right: Castle No 5045 *Earl of Dudley* at Ranelagh Road, Paddington.

Right: A Birkenhead train is headed out of Paddington by King class 4-6-0
No 6011 *King James I.*

Some 4-4-0s

Above: The up 'Thames-Clyde Express' leaves Leeds City for St Pancras; Class 4P 4-4-0 No 41096 pilots a Class 5 4-6-0.

Top right: Ex-LNWR 4-4-0 No 25321 *Lord Loch* at Wavertree.

Right: Precursor 4-4-0 No 25310 heads a Liverpool to Holyhead train at Wavertree.

Below: Schools Class 4-4-0 No 30916 *Whitgift* at Hildenborough with an up Hastings train.

Right: SR Class E 4-4-0 No 1273 near Hildenborough with a train from Hastings.

Bottom right: Class L 4-4-0 No 1773 heads a summer excursion to the Kent Coast out of Victoria.

Up the Hill from Kings Cross

Above: An evening train to Leeds and Bradford, headed by Class A1 Pacific No 60117 *Bois Rousel*.

Right: The down Flying Scotsman approaches Copenhagen Tunnel with A4 Pacific No 60014 *Silver Link* in charge.

Thompson Class A1 Pacific No 60158 *Aberdonian* with a down Newcastle train passes Class A4 Pacific No 60031 *Golden Plover,* waiting to back down to Kings Cross for duty with down 'Elizabethan'.

Above: A morning train for Leeds and Bradford passes Copenhagen box, hauled by Class A4 Pacific No 60017 *Silver Fox.*

Left: A morning train to Glasgow from Kings Cross enters Gasworks Tunnel behind Class A2 Pacific No 60532 *Blue Peter.*

Liverpool

The up 'Merseyside Express' rounds the curve at Wavertree behind Stanier
Pacific No 6232 *Duchess of Montrose.*

Above: Un-rebuilt Scot No 6112 *Sherwood Forester* leans to the curve past Edge Hill sheds with the up 'Merseyside Express'.

Top right: A Liverpool to West of England train at Wavertree, headed by Princess Pacific No 6201 *Princess Elizabeth*.

Right: The only steam engine without cylinders. Turbomotive No 6202 pulls away from Mossley Hill with the up 'Merseyside Express'.

Streamline Era

Above: The up 'Coronation Scot' at Boar's Head, hauled by Princess Coronation Class Pacific No 6223 *Princess Alice.*

Top right: The pre-war down 'Yorkshire Pullman' passes Hadley Wood with Class A4 Pacific No 4900 *Gannet.*

Right: One of the eight streamlined 4-6-4s of the SNCF Nord Region, four cylinder compound No 232 5 002, at the Gard du Nord, Paris.

Above: The pre-war down 'Flying Scotsman' passes Finsbury Park behind Class A4 Pacific No 4489 *Dominion of Canada.*

Below: The down 'Coronation Scot' at Boar's Head near Wigan with Princess Coronation Pacific No 6223 *Princess Alice.*

Carlisle-Border City

Above: The down 'Waverley' express about to leave for Edinburgh behind class A3 Pacific No 60087 *Blenheim.*

Top right: Locomotive exchange at Carlisle. Stanier Pacific No 46231 *Duchess of Atholl* waits to take over the down 'Royal Scot' which has arrived from the south behind No 46244 *King George VI.*

Right: Class A3 Pacific No 60097 *Humorist* at Canal Junction with the down 'Waverley' express. This was the first engine of its class to be fitted with double chimney and smoke deflectors.

Above: Afternoon Parade at Carlisle. Stanier Pacific No 46244 *King George VI* brings in a Scottish express from the south, to be taken forward by Princess Pacific No 46201 *Princess Elizabeth.* 'Jubilee' 4-6-0 No 45724 *Warspite* awaits a train for Perth from Euston.

Left: Princess Elizabeth and *Warspite* await their turn of duty at Citadel station.

Top right: Stanier Pacific No 46255 *City of Hereford* leaves Carlisle with a Birmingham to Glasgow train. On the right is 'Jinty' 0-6-0T No 47492.

Right: A Euston to Perth train at Kingmoor, north of Carlisle, behind Princess Pacific No 46203 *Princess Margaret Rose.*

Leeds - Railway Capital of West Riding

Above: Nice bit of exhaust on the Whitehall curve! Jubilee 4-6-0 No 45640 *Frobisher* pilots rebuilt Scot No 46133 *The Green Howards* on the down 'Thames-Clyde Express'.

Top right: The up 'Yorkshire Pullman' at Beeston, headed by Class A3 Pacific No 60047 *Donovan.*

Right: The up 'Queen of Scots' rounds the bend at Holbeck as it approaches Leeds Central. Class A3 Pacific No 60084 *Trigo* is in charge.

Light and shade at Leeds City. Class A4 Pacific No 60026 *Miles Beevor* sets out for London with the up 'Yorkshire Pullman'.

Below: One of the A3s allotted to Holbeck, No 60038 *Firdaussi* at Wortley Junction with the down 'Thames-Clyde Express'.

Right: Compound 4-4-0 No 41063 assists a Jubilee 4-6-0 with the up 'Thames-Clyde Express' from Leeds City station.

Bottom right: Class 4MT 4-6-0 No 75062 leaves Leeds City with a Bristol to Bradford train. Jubilee 4-6-0 No 45724 *Warspite* waits to take the down 'Waverley' forward from Leeds.

Over the Border

Above: The morning train from Fort William to Glasgow steams out in the rain behind Class K2 2-6-0s No 61787 *Loch Quoich* and No 61772 *Loch Lochy.*

Top right: The down 'Elizabethan' at Portobello East Junction, headed by A4 Pacific No 60012 *Commonwealth of Australia.*

Right: Class J25 0-6-0 No 65667 shunting in the Portobello goods yard.

Above: A Perth train approaches Beattock Summit, hauled by Class 5MT 4-6-0 No 45161.

Below: Class K4 2-6-0 No 61996 *Lord of the Isles* on a West Highland freight train in the Monessie Gorge.

PRIVATE ENTERPRISE
Keighley and Worth Valley

Above: Ex-GWR and later LPTB 0-6-0PT No 5775 leaves Haworth with a train for Oxenhope.

Right: Ex-USA 0-6-0T No 72 darkens the sky at Haworth on a dull winter's day.

Above: Ex-NCB 0-6-0T *Fred* shunts at Haworth.

Top right: Ex-NCB 0-6-0ST *Fred* and another 0-6-0ST, No 62, in Haworth yard.

Right: Crewe-built 2-6-2T No 41241 approaches Oxenhope.

Above: Class 5MT No 5025 approaches Oxenhope station. This locomotive is in the ownership of Mr W. E. C. Watkinson and will eventually work on the Strathspey Railway in Scotland.

Left: Ex-BR 2-6-2T No 41241 takes water at Keighley station.

Right: The 2-6-2T No 41241 emerges from Mytholmes Tunnel with an afternoon train.

Below: The ex-GWR and LPTB 0-6-0PT rounds the bend from Keighley station and starts the climb to Haworth.

Below: Class 5 4-6-0 No 45212 crosses the Mytholme Viaduct between Oakworth and Haworth.

Right: An 0-6-0ST, No 62, built by Robert Stephenson & Hawthorns passes a typical Yorkshire mill building on the approaches to Haworth station.

Bottom right: A typical scene in Haworth yard.

Top left: Class 5 4-6-0S Nos 5025 and 45212 ready for departure.

Left: The 0-6-0T *Fred* gives footplate rides at Haworth.

Above: Ex-US Army 0-6-0T No 72 passes Ingrow station in a shower of rain.

The 'Flying Scotsman'

Above: Flying Scotsman leaves Wakefield Kirkgate with an excursion to Llandudno.

Top right: On a freezing day, Gresley Pacific No 4472 *Flying Scotsman* at Doncaster.

Right: Contrast in front ends: *Flying Scotsman* and Brush diesel No 5586 at Doncaster.

Bluebell Railway

Above: 0-6-0 No 27 (ex-SECR) leaves Sheffield Park with a train for Horsted Keynes.

Top right: A Bluebell railway train with 0-6-0 No 27 in charge stands at Sheffield Park.

Right: 0-6-0 No 27 leaves Horsted Keynes with a train for Sheffield Park.

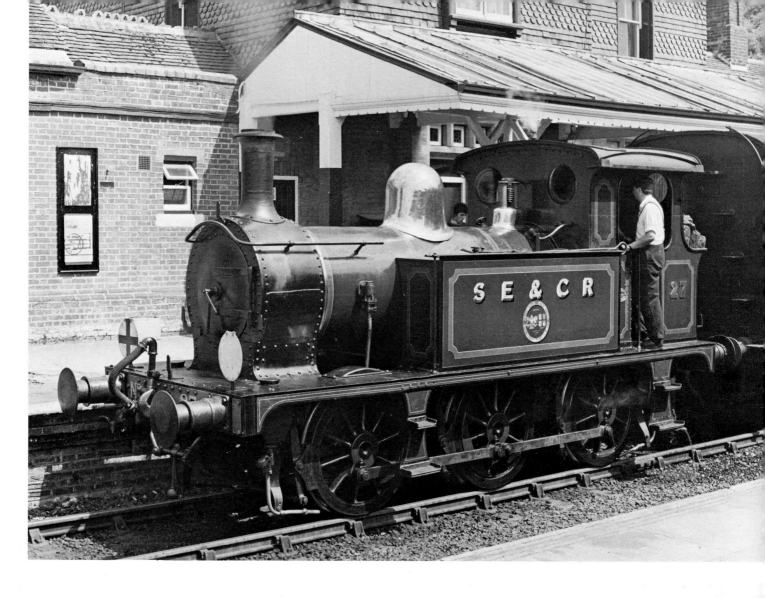

North Yorkshire Moors

Above: View at Grosmont station as 0-6-2T No 5 (Ex-NCB Philadelphia) sets out for the summit. Class Q6 0-8-0 No 3395 waits in the station bay.

Right: 0-6-2T No 29, Ex-NCB Philadelphia, sets out from Grosmont with a train for the summit at Ellerbeck.

Top left: Ex-NER Class P3 0-6-0 No 2392 undergoes preparation at Grosmont.

Left: 0-6-2T No 29 *Lambton* backs its train into Grosmont station.

Above: Another picture of No 29 as it gets away from Grosmont with a summer afternoon train.

Far left: P3 No 2392 blasts its way up the hill to Goathland from Grosmont.

Left: Intimate view of 0-6-2T No 29 *Lambton* at Grosmont.

Bottom left: Goathland station. No 5 and No 29 with the little 0-4-0 *Mirvale* in the background.

Below: No 29 *Lambton* and P3 No 2392 back down to the station at Grosmont.

Above: Class P3 0-6-0 No 2392 at Grosmont.

Top right: No 2392 at Ellerbeck Summit with the Fylingdale's early warning equipment in the background.

Right: No 2392 at Beckfoot.

Above: The 0-6-2 No 5 at Grosmont.

Top right: No 29 *Lambton* rounds the curve to the west of Grosmont.

Right: No 29 backs on to its train at Grosmont.

Another view of No 5 as it emerges from the tunnel at Grosmont with a train for Goathland.

185

Severn Valley

Above: North of Eardington WD 0-6-0T No 193 heads for Bridgnorth.

Top right: The day that No 193 arrived at Bridgnorth: unloading from the 'low-loader'.

Right: WD 0-6-0T No 193 is manhandled in the yard at Bridgnorth.

Above: Hand coaling No 193 a few hours after its arrival at Bridgnorth.

Top right: Collett 0-6-0 No 3205 and WD 2-10-0 No 600 *Gordon* at Bridgnorth.

Right: The ex-GWR, later Ex-LPTB 0-6-0PT No 5764 is coaled at Bridgnorth.

Tyseley

Castle class 4-6-0 No 7029 *Clun Castle* on the turntable in Tyseley shed
(those streaks are rain pouring in through the shed roof).

Above: Clun Castle at Wortley Junction, leaves with an excursion for Carlisle.

Below: Jubilee 4-6-0 No 5593 *Kolhapur* in steam at Tyseley.

Left: Inside the new shed at Tyseley with ex-LSWR Class T9 4-4-0 No 120 and Horwich-built ex-L&Y 2-4-2T No 1008 in the foreground.

Bottom left: May 3rd, 1969. Preparing the nameplate *Eric Treacy* of Class 5 4-6-0 No 5428 for unveiling by the Bishop of Birmingham.

Below: Kolhapur and *Clun Castle* on an exhibition run for the BBC cameras in October 1970.

Top left: Stanier Jubilee 4-6-0
No 5593 *Kolhapur.*

Left: Castle Class 4-6-0 No 7029
Clun Castle.

Above: Stanier Black 5 No 5428
Eric Treacy on the day of the naming
ceremony.

Right: The nameplate of No 5428.

Top left: Clun Castle in steam at Tyseley.

Left: In procession at Tyseley, *Clun Castle* leads King Arthur 4-6-0
No 777 *Sir Lamiel,* a Peckett 0-4-0T, 2-4-2T No 1008, and Class T9 4-4-0
No 120.

Above: Kolhapur does a bit of slipping at Tyseley.

'King George V' at Hereford

'King class No 6000 *King George V* in its shed at Bulmer's Cider Works, Hereford.

The 'Hereford Pullman'. No 6000 *King George V* hauls the Pullman
coaches in Bulmer's private sidings.

Day's work over, the King is propelled back to its shed.

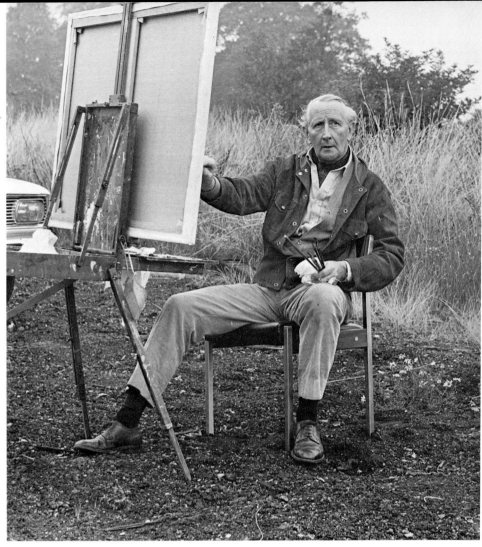

Two views of Terence Cuneo painting
King George V at Hereford.

Steamtown, Carnforth

Photographed from the coaling stage at Carnforth is Stanier Class 5
4-6-0 No 44871.

Left: Bank Holiday at Carnforth with three locomotives in steam.

Right: Class B1 4-6-0 No 61306 *Mayflower* hauls a brake-van at Carnforth.

Below: Early morning at Carnforth shed. Stanier 4-6-0 No 44871 and 2-6-0 No 6441 are raising steam.

Chapelon Pacific No 231 K 22 in process of repainting.

Lightweight and heavyweight: 2-6-0 No 6441 and the Chapelon Pacific.

Bahamas Society, Dinting

In perfect condition, Jubilee 4-6-0 No 5596 *Bahamas* in steam at Dinting.

Class A4 Pacific No 4498 *Sir Nigel Gresley* threads York station with an
excursion to Newcastle.